A year *in the life of bindi

A year *in the life of bindi

RANDOM HOUSE AUSTRALIA

A Random House book
Published by Random House Australia Pty Ltd
Level 3, 100 Pacific Highway, North Sydney NSW 2060
www.randomhouse.com.au

First published by Random House Australia in 2011

Copyright © Australia Zoo 2011

The moral right of the authors has been asserted.

Addresses for companies within the Random House Group can be found at
www.randomhouse.com.au/offices

National Library of Australia
Cataloguing-in-Publication entry

Author: Black, Jess
Title: A Year in the Life of Bindi / Jess Black and Bindi Irwin
ISBN: 978 1 86471 838 6 (pbk.)
Target Audience: For children
Subjects: Irwin, Bindi, 1998–
Other Authors/Contributors: Irwin, Bindi, 1998–
Dewey Number: 333.72092

Front cover photograph © Getty Images
Back cover photographs © Australia Zoo
Cover, internal design and typesetting by Liz Seymour, Seymour Designs
All internal photographs © Australia Zoo, except for photo on p40 © Getty Images

Printed by 1010 Printing International Limited

10 9 8 7 6 5 4 3 2 1

MIX
Paper from
responsible sources
FSC® C016973
www.fsc.org

The FSC® Logo identifies products which contain wood
from well managed forests certified in accordance with
the rules of the Forest Stewardship Council.

CONTENTS

CONTENTS

JULY JULY JULY JULY JULY JULY JULY JULY JULY JULY JULY JULY JULY JULY

JULY JULY JULY

I had the best 12th birthday ever! Hollywood came to Australia Zoo on 24 July, my birthday. It was amazing; I got to dress up, spend time with my friends and family and have fun. I rode in a pink stretch hummer all the way to the pink carpet where my mum, brother, his best friend Riley and my best friend Rosie strutted down. That was unbelievable! It was so nice of Tania Zaetta, Jamie Dunn and Agro, Dawn Fraser, Senator Mark Furner, Carolyn Male MP, Aaron Harvie and Denise Morcombe to come and walk down the pink carpet too. You guys rock! Then Mum and I fed the crocs in frocks. That's right, we were in our dresses feeding the croc. Wes was even in his suit while feeding. However, I think one of the best parts of the day was seeing and eating my incredible Hollywood / Free Willy: Escape from Pirates Cove cake. WOW! Lastly, a giant thank-you to everyone who came for my birthday – you made the day so wonderful. I hope to see you all again next year.

MY BIRTHDAY

theme HOLLYWOOD

③

Whale watching Launch

Whale watching season is always such a fun time of year. It starts in July and ends in November when the whales head south. On *Steve's Whale One* anyone can go out to watch and enjoy these gentle giants of the ocean. They are amazing! Sometimes they come right up to the boat and breach. Did you know whales burn around 3000 calories every time they breach? My mum, Robert and I always have fun launching *Steve's Whale One* every year. It's great for people to see and learn about these gorgeous creatures because they are in a lot of trouble. People need to remember to never buy any wildlife products. When the buying stops the killing can too!

Steve's Whale One

Think of chocolate, Tasmanian devils and one of the most gorgeous mountains in the world. Well, you're probably thinking of Tasmania. We got to go to the yummy House of Anvers chocolate factory in Latrobe, where I ate loads of incredible chocolate and got to see how they make it. Very interesting. Then we went to check up on the gorgeous Tasmanian devils. You see they are suffering from a facial tumour disease, which is one of only two known contagious cancers. They need all the help they can get. We then got to see and climb the stunning Cradle Mountain. Beautiful and a bit cold.

Agnes the River Turtle*

Agnes is an adult female Brisbane River Turtle who was admitted to the Australia Zoo Wildlife Hospital suffering serious injuries to her carapace (the top of her shell). Agnes was one of fifty-eight Brisbane River turtles rescued back in March from a dam about 30km west of Brisbane. A member of the public had been visiting the dam and noticed a small pond at the base of the spillway wall, crowded with turtles. The turtles had been carried over the spillway wall when excess water had been released; sadly some had been injured or killed while others were left isolated in a small pond surrounded by rocks.

Agnes, weighing a thin 1.59kg, was assessed by Dr Amber on arrival. She found that Agnes had fractured segments along the front and rear edge of her carapace and a deep 4cm wide hole in the top of her carapace. Agnes was lucky her spine hadn't been fractured or any organs ruptured. Dr Amber placed Agnes under anaesthetic to debride (remove dead tissue) and clean all of Agnes's wounds. The damaged rear edge of the carapace also needed to be trimmed and the skin sutured closed. The hole needed to be covered in medicated ointment and protected by a bandage, and Agnes was also placed on pain relief and antibiotic treatment. Bandage changes were scheduled for every second day and importantly the wound was not to get wet, so Agnes was only allowed to be in shallow water while feeding and then returned to a dry enclosure.

Agnes now weighs a healthy 1.91kg and she is feeding and swimming normally, so Dr Amber sent Agnes into care with a reptile rehabilitator for the remainder of the winter period. After a final health check in spring Agnes was cleared to return back home to the wild.

Happy Birthday to...
Mia the Dingo

* Age: 11 years (DOB 27/7/1999)
* Gender: Female
* Mia is the littermate of Kirra and Cooya. She is now the alpha female of Group Four and has three juvenile dingos in her pack. Mia is the most shy of the three older girls, but has enough personality to become dominant over the three juveniles. Mia is easy to distinguish as she is very light in colour and has a lot of white on her face. She loves to run and play with the rest of the girls, and all four can be seen racing around the exhibit, running through the creek or swimming in the pond. Mia loves meeting the guests who participate in the Animal Encounters, and is quite happy to just lie in the grass and allow everyone to pat and admire her.

AUGUST
AUGUST
AUGUST
AUGUST
AUGUST
AUGUST
AUGUST
AUGUST
AUGUST
AUGUST
AUGUST
AUGUST
AUGUST
AUGUST
AUGUST
AUGUST
AUGUST

AUGUST AUGUST AUGUST

Camping rocks! I reckon the best place in the world to camp is at my dad's reserve. We have a place there called 'Bull Shark Camp', that we call home for one month every year on our crocodile research trips. It was called that because of the stunning bull sharks in the Wenlock River. They're so cute. Sometimes if you're really lucky you may see one cruising up the river. However there are many other local residents in the camp. We get visited by breathtaking birds, fruit bats, cuscus, spiders, snakes, and huge bright green frogs in the shower, orchestras of crickets at night and lots more. One time I caught a skink and it bit my nose and started to death roll. Hilarious! I think it thought it was a 16-foot crocodile. I also like to sit and swing in the camp hammock. It's especially fun to grab a good book and read in the hammock. Very relaxing. For brekky, usually it's jaffles. We toast them on the fire. Yuuuuummy! Then, at night I like to help prepare dinner. Camp food is always the best food.

Camp Croc

The croc trip is all about . . . you guessed it . . . crocs! Nobody knows a lot about them, where they go or what they get up too. Our research trip aims to answer those questions. This year Mum got to help Professor Craig Franklin insert acoustic trackers into crocodiles. The trackers tell the body temperature of the crocodile, where it swims within the river system and what depth it dives to. Then Mum got to perform the operation with Professor Franklin on a croc all on her own. She did so well. I'm very proud of her! Sometimes on very lucky crocodiles we attach satellite trackers. This can tell us where they are anywhere in the world. It is very interesting, but the more we learn the more questions we have. I'm probably the luckiest sister in the world! I can't believe that Robert and I jumped our first crocodile together by ourselves. He is amazing! Robert jumped the head and I took the rest of the croc. I'm so proud of him. What a great team effort! We got to jump more than one beautiful croc together. I have memories that will stay with me forever.

13

Hoot the Southern Boobook Owl

One night in August, staff at the Australia Zoo Wildlife Hospital received a call for help regarding an injured owl that had been found in Mooloolah Valley. Anne, the lady who rescued the owl, had been driving home at dusk when she saw it sitting on the side of the road being surrounded and attacked by other birds.

She called the Australia Zoo Wildlife Hospital, directions were given and within half an hour Hoot the southern boobook owl was receiving veterinary treatment for a painful eye injury and concussion.

Dr Claude assessed Hoot and took X-rays, which fortunately showed no fractures. Hoot's eye had a corneal ulcer with edema around it (meaning an injury to the surface of the eye surrounded by an abnormal build up of fluid) plus a mild perforation to the side of the eye.

Hoot was initially prescribed pain relief, sub-cutaneous fluids and medicated eye ointment, plus plenty of food and rest in the Bird Intensive Care.

Since admittance Hoot has had four veterinary rechecks and so far there has been a marked improvement in the eye's condition. As with any wild bird of prey, perfect eyesight is essential so they can hunt for food effectively; if one eye is permanently damaged, release and long-term survival prospects aren't good, but the AZWH will make sure he has a good life, whether or not he can be released into the wild.

Happy Birthday to...
Carly the Goat

* Age: 2 years (DOB 27/08/2008)
* Gender: Female
* Carly is an Anglo-Nubian Cross. She is a very pretty goat with long ears and a mournful cry. Carly has lots of personality and is very clever and inquisitive. Don't let her appearance fool you – she is very coordinated and has great balance and climbing skills. Carly loves to get brushed and will often come over so guests can scratch her on the head or legs, but be careful if you bend down to give her a pat, you may get a kiss on the cheek or a nibble on the ear!

SEPTEMBER SEPTEMBER

The Simpson Desert was a perfect place to take some beaut photos. Because I am interested in photography it was fun trying to take interesting pics around the desert. I got some funky shots of flowers blooming, lush green trees, the red sand and even some of Robert. One of the

pictures I used in an art essay for school. My teacher really liked it because she said the photo had meaning.

I can't get over what a wildlife hotspot the Simpson Desert is! Mum, Robert, Wes, his parents Dawn and Ray, Shelley, Barry, Hannah and I had a blast. We sprinted for a sand goanna, Wes tossed a fierce snake, which is the most venomous snake on earth, and Robert caught heaps of bearded dragons and moved them off the road. Wes caught a perentie, which was so cute. I made friends with a friendly echidna and saw so much more. We looked around caves and found animal skeletons that Robert had fun piecing together. We saw bird eggs that were going to hatch and some little chicks that had only been out of the egg for a little while. They looked like balls of cotton with tiny black eyes. Gorgeous.

A DESERT ADVENTURE

We didn't just have a great time while we were out looking for wildlife; our camp was a pretty fun place too. Every night we'd all sit around the fire eating dinner and telling some very funny stories. One night Wes' dad, Ray, broke out his guitar for a campfire sing-a-long! That was a lot of fun. Another memory I'll never forget is having a bath in the dam. The water was knee-deep and freezing. I've never been so cold. It was hilarious, because everyone in the camp heard my yelps and screams as I tried to wash in the ice-cold water. Haha! At least I'll remember it and they'll never stop teasing me about it. In the camp Robert and I were lucky enough to have a school tent. Every day before heading out, Robert and I did three hours of school. It felt strange to be learning about politics in the middle of the Simpson Desert.

21

Chance the Brown Goshawk

In September, the Australia Zoo Rescue Unit received a call for help from the staff at RSL Care Buderim regarding an injured brown goshawk. The bird was discovered lying on a third floor verandah and appeared to be extremely unwell, so he was rushed to the Australia Zoo Wildlife Hospital for emergency veterinary treatment.

The brown goshawk, who had been named Chance, was in a bad way – he couldn't even stand. Dr Tania discovered his oral cavity (mouth) and trachea (wind pipe) were full of blood. He also had severe bruising and a hematoma (build-up of leaked blood) on the right jugular (a large vein that returns blood to the heart from the head and neck). It was an intense time for the veterinary team, as twice while under anaesthetic Chance's heart stopped beating and he had to be revived with an injection of adrenaline; fortunately he responded both times.

The next day Chance was upright and perching. He still had his right eye closed but his overall condition was definitely improving. Four days after being admitted Chance was eating on his own and starting to fly short distances.

Dr Tania has since made the decision to transfer Chance to Currumbin Sanctuary's large flight aviary where he can regain his flight strength and fitness, prior to release back in the Buderim area.

Brown goshawks are by nature shy and secretive birds; they will sit quietly among foliage and then emerge to ambush their prey, which might be a bird, small mammal, reptile or even a large insect.

Happy Birthday to...
Nuebi the Barking Owl

* Age: 5 years (DOB 30/9/2005)
* Gender: Male
* Nuebi is our very handsome barking owl that just loves a good scratch. He gets super excited before flying in our 'Bird of Prey' show and just loves to fly through the crowd. He is an extremely agile flyer, and while flying close above the audiences' heads, everyone gets a chance to look into his bright yellow eyes.

  Nuebi is able to turn his head 270 degrees in either direction and almost upside down. This is because those amazing yellow eyes are fixed in his head and he needs to be able to turn that head to see what's going on around him. That's why he has 14 vertebra in his neck, compared with humans, who only have 7. If you're lucky you might even get to hear him bark!

25

OCTOBER
OCTOBER

What a SENSATIONAL day we had at Universal Studios! I almost got eaten by Jaws the shark (I wish he still lived in the water)! We also got to go on the exciting Jurassic Park ride. Robert loved that and wanted to keep going on it all day. I got to meet the gorgeous Marilyn Monroe and visit the cutest Betty Boop store. My mum was in heaven in there! However, the most memorable thing about Universal Studios was their Halloween festivities. Very scary! It still has Robert a bit freaked out.

UNIVERSAL FUN!

WASHINGTON DC, USA

IN THIS TEMPLE
AS IN THE HEARTS OF THE PEOPLE
FOR WHOM HE SAVED THE UNION
THE MEMORY OF ABRAHAM LINCOLN
IS ENSHRINED FOREVER

Washington DC was a very interesting place to visit; it has a lot of political history to learn about. While we were there we visited the Lincoln Memorial, and saw the Washington Monument and the White House. However I reckon the best place we went to was a small park with some nuts and bread. We got to feed some gorgeous ducks and squirrels. The squirrels even sat on our laps to eat the nuts we had. It was tip-top terrific.

HALLOWEEN, USA

How much fun is Halloween in America?

It's AWESOME!! You get to dress up and knock on people's doors saying 'Trick or treat'. Then they give you lollies or chocolate. We spent Halloween with friends in New York. I dressed up as a spooky vampire and Robert was a beaut bonza chef. I loved having fangs – they were so cool! I kept scaring people, which was very funny. You should see how some people decorate their backyards and houses. It's like how Australians decorate their houses for Christmas. Robert couldn't get over the fact that people just give you lollies and chocolate. He kept asking us, 'Are you sure I can just take the lollies?' He is very cute. I hope that we can go back to America for Halloween next year because it was so much fun.

Emmett the Tawny Frogmouth Fledgling*

A call from staff at Dakabin RSPCA shelter came through asking for an assessment of a tawny frogmouth with a possible wing injury. A member of the public named Brett had picked up the fledgling after it was blown out of its nest during high winds.

Emmett was transferred to the Australia Zoo Wildlife Hospital to receive a full medical assessment. Fortunately this revealed no injuries or fractures, so Emmett was given a clean bill of health and arrangements were made to get him back home to his parents.

Megan from the Australia Zoo Wildlife Hospital transported Emmett back down to Deception Bay where she was met by Brett the rescuer. The release went very well, probably helped by the fact that tawny frogmouth are nocturnal birds. Brett promised to check on Emmett each day as he went on his morning walk and contact us if anything went wrong . . . but so far, so good.

Happy Birthday to...
Goliath the Aldabran Tortoise

❋ Age: 34 years (DOB 9/10/1976)
❋ Gender: Male
❋ Goliath, as the name suggests, is big. But he doesn't just have a big shell, he has a big heart too. Goliath is, without a doubt, the coolest and trendiest out of all the giant tortoises at Australia Zoo. With his ochre-stained scutes, which are shaped like pyramids, he looks like a mobile Egyptian landscape. As soon as Goliath sees you enter his home and acreage, he sprints over to you as fast as those round tortoise legs will take him (not that he goes that fast – he is a tortoise after all!). When he finally roaches his destination it becomes his priority to absorb as much of your attention as possible. He ensures that an ample amount of scratches and rubs are given to meet his goliath quota.

33

Canberra's War Memorial is such an eye-opening and important place for Australia. I was lucky enough to visit the memorial with my mum, Robert and friends. I was deeply moved by the stories told there. I would have never known what went on just to keep us safe and our country free. I realised what we take for granted and just how lucky we are. It is unbelievable to think of all the lives lost and the pain that the soldiers and their families went through. I'm extraordinarily grateful and hope that more people will visit the memorial.

THIS IS YOUR LIFE

I'm so proud of my mum. She is such an amazing person and I hope to be like her when I grow up. When Eddie McGuire came out into the Crocoseum to tell Mum that she was going to be on *This Is Your Life,* her face said it all. It was so funny to see how surprised she was and I was so happy for her. We flew down to Melbourne where the show was filmed and Mum got surprised by her friends and family. It was a great night.

LADY ELLIOT ISLAND

Lady Elliot Island is one of my favourite places in the world. There are so many things that you can do. My best friend came out with us and we got to do heaps of stand-up paddle boarding and snorkelling. While I was there I even got to try scuba diving for the first time with friends. Wow! Lady Elliot Island is part of the Great Barrier Reef, which means that there is some sensational underwater life. It was so much fun being able to breathe underwater down with all the fantastic turtles, fish, coral, sharks and more. I loved it! However, the wildlife doesn't just stay in the water. We got to see some turtles nesting on the beach and most of the birds on the island had eggs that were going to hatch soon. We all had such a great time!

Hardy the Rufous Bettong

A male Rufous Bettong was found at Nanango in the South Burnett Region after being hit by a car. On assessment it was revealed he was suffering a fracture to his big toe on the right hind foot. X-rays were taken and a cast was applied to immobilise the fracture site. Pain relief and anti-inflammatories were prescribed.

The cast was removed after a few weeks and X-rayed again to establish the fracture had healed. Hardy should make a full recovery.

Rufous Bettongs are nocturnal. They collect grass and sticks to make nests, and carry the collected materials with their prehensile tail.

Happy Birthday to...
Agro the Saltwater Crocodile

* Age: 33 years (DOB 11/11/1977)
* Gender: Male
* Length: 4.6m (14.72ft)
* Agro is one impressive croc. He was captured from the wild back in 1988. My dad removed him from Cattle Creek in north Queensland to protect him from being shot dead by hunters.

  Agro is now very happy protecting his new territory, a freshwater billabong here at Australia Zoo! Not only is Agro protecting his waterhole, he is also extremely protective of a beautiful female crocodile, Sheila. The love of his life is Cookie, a large female of 10ft who was caught in exactly the same area as Agro, so these two were probably a bit of an item in the wild. She has a beautiful nature, the quietest and gentlest of all our crocodiles. Agro and Cookie are a perfect couple; they get on like a house on fire.

41

DECEMBER DECEMBER DECEMBER

Every year we go out and visit two of our conservation properties, one on the Great Dividing Range and one on the Brigalow Belt, in Queensland. We always have such a good time looking for wildlife and this year Robert brought his motorbike, so he had a blast riding around on that. We got to go and visit friends out there and they let me have a ride on their horse, Johnny Wilkinson. That was so much fun. I also enjoyed swimming in the dam, hugging the emus and tracking Chili, one of the woma pythons that we are researching. The managers of the property have seven kids, two of whom are around my age. It is always fun to hang out with them. Jesse and I went on our first camping trip alone, which was awesome! We cooked sausages on a campfire and had a ball.

A fun girls' night! I look forward to going out there again soon.

AN OUTBACK VISIT

BIRTHDAY BOY

My little brother is dinosaur mad; he lives and breathes dinosaurs. I love him very much and I'm always learning from him. When his birthday comes around it is dinotastic! Erth Dinosaurs came to the zoo, we had *Prehistoric Park* playing on the big screen in the Crocoseum, and even a real life palaeontologist from the Queensland Museum was talking to people about dinosaurs. I can't believe that Robert is 7 already and I'm so lucky that he is the best brother in the world.

WINTON
500 Km

Happy 7th Birthday Robe

OPRAH

I'm so proud that Oprah came here, to Australia, for three special shows! I think that Australia is the most gorgeous and diverse place on the planet. We've got stunning oceans and beaches and spectacular outback areas! We were so honoured when she asked us to be on her show in Sydney at the Opera House, when she came Down Under. The first time I was on the Oprah Show was when I was about three years old, with my mum and dad. Robert wasn't even thought of yet! We had a great time with her, showing off some stunning wildlife, and some she was not too keen on! This time we flew to Sydney from our property on the Brigalow Belt. Mum, Robert and I all walked out on stage together with a woma python and an olive python. They were very cute; and I was very proud of Oprah for overcoming her fear of snakes! It was a great day and I'm so glad that we got to share our conservation message with a lot of people.

45

Frodo the Baby Koala

Frodo the baby koala was found at Jimna, near Kenilworth and transported to the Australia Zoo Wildlife Hospital by the Australia Zoo Rescue Unit.

It was found she had a fractured skull and significant damage to the stomach and intestines as a result of being shot with what appears to be the spray of a shot gun. X-rays revealed approximately 15 pellets scattered throughout her body.

Frodo required an immediate blood transfusion, intravenous antibiotics, fluids and strong pain relief. Two surgeries have been completed, removing a total of seven pellets.

Frodo is recovering extremely well. She is now eating leaves on her own, moving around her outdoor enclosure and has also gained some weight. Frodo is expected to stay in hospital for a minimum of six to eight months. Sustaining these injuries as a 2kg koala makes the road to recovery tougher. The biggest worry at the moment is the possibility that she may succumb to lead toxicity as some of the pellets remain in her intestinal tract.

Happy Birthday to...
Maneki the Sumatran Tiger

* Age: 3 years (DOB 4/12/2007)
* Gender: Female
* Weight: 81kg (178.2lbs)
* Maneki was born at Taman Safari Indonesia and spent three months there with our handlers before making her way to Australia Zoo. Just like her brother Bashii and sister Kaitlyn, Maneki was named by a guest through Australia Zoo's online auction. Her name comes from a Japanese phrase 'Maneki Neko' which means Good Luck Cat. Proceeds from the auction went into active projects in Sumatra to protect wild Sumatran tigers from illegal poachers. Maneki is very affectionate towards her handlers, which is a big change from that little cub who enjoyed chewing on her handlers every chance she had.

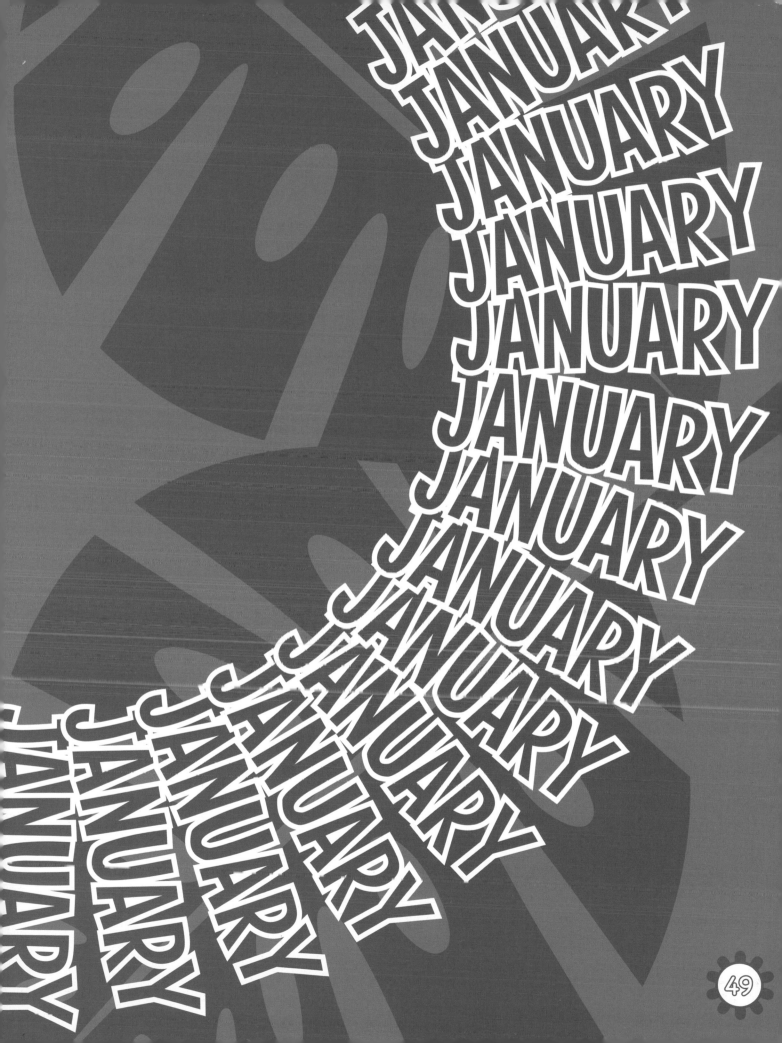

49

JANUARY JANUARY JANUARY

Our family celebrates half birthdays where we just have our closest friends and family come, because our real birthdays can be quite busy. We call it our un-birthday. Wow! What can I say? I have never been so surprised and happy in my life. I had forgotten that I was twelve and a half, so everyone totally surprised me with an un-birthday party. However, I think the biggest surprise was seeing my two friends, Rosie, who came up from Ipswich, and missed the first day of school, and Harley, who came down from Katherine, and missed the first week of school. Thank you! I couldn't believe my eyes when I saw them – I think I did a double take. My cake was stunning; it had my favourite animal on it – an echidna. It was delicious too! It was really nice of everyone to come and put the celebration together. I love them all so much and wouldn't be the person I am today without them.

CROC AND JUNGLE GIRLS SHOWS

School holidays at the zoo are always so much fun! I love them because I get to do the shows with the Jungle Girls and croc shows with Wes, Mum and Robert. This year's shows were better than ever. It was great to see all of the kids dancing along while the Jungle Girls and I performed in the Crocoseum.

Then when Mum, Wes and Robert and I did the croc shows, the crocs always went off. I think that the shows are their favourite part of the day too. On Australia Day, for our last show, Mum and Wes surprised me. They told me that I'd be taking over Mum's part of the show. Wes is a great teacher and I really look up to him; he helped me through the show. It was a fantastic day that I'll never forget!

52

Harley Tour

It was a lot of fun showing our friends from Katherine Australia Zoo this week. We threw them in with all the animals. I loved taking Dawn, Riley, Holly, Harley and David in with the rhino, lemurs and giraffes. I also got to take Harley and Dawn in with one of our tigers, Bashii. Did you know tigers have stripes imprinted on their skin too? Harley and I also got to go in with one of our gorgeous komodo dragons and our three sweet Asian elephants, Siam, Sabu and little Bimbo.

Diva the Gould's Long-eared Bat

A gorgeous micro bat was admitted and was identified as a Gould's Long-eared bat. Even though she is a fully grown female, she weighed only nine grams.

The micro bat, named Diva, was dehydrated and suffering an injury to her left wing, which was preventing her from flying. X-rays taken showed the wing wasn't fractured, just badly bruised, which is lucky for Diva. Diva has been placed in care with the licensed carer who rescued her and is expected to make a full recovery.

Micro bats are nocturnal mammals, sleeping through the day in tree hollows, under loose bark and sometimes buildings. These roost sites are also used to rear young and sleep when inactive over the colder months, sometimes housing up to 25 bats in a single colony.

Gould's Long-eared bats typically fly close to the ground when hunting to catch airborne insects or insects on the ground or on vegetation, then eating the insect while continuing to fly. All micro bats are natural pest controllers, consuming half their body weight per night in insects. Without the many micro bat species in the environment we would be plagued by insects.

Happy Birthday to...
Wendy the Wombat

* Age: 1 year (DOB 19/1/2010)
* Gender: Female
* Wendy is bursting with character. She certainly takes on her mother's sweet nature and her father's cheeky antics. You can catch her taste-testing all sorts of objects whether they are edible or not, scampering about awkwardly, still learning to coordinate her clumsy legs in time with each other. Of course now that she is so big she can hardly fit in Minibus' pouch and because wombats have a backwards-facing pouch, you can sometimes spot an arm, leg or head hanging out.

57

FEBRUARY FEBRUARY FEBRUARY

Uluru is the heart of Australia and such a beautiful place to visit. The area is usually called the Red Centre, however after all the rain these past couple of years, I think it should be renamed the green centre! There are bushes sprouting everywhere, flowers blooming and the wildlife is loving it. Every day, around where we were staying, Robert would try really hard to catch sand goannas. He always came close, but was never quite fast enough. When you get to see Uluru up close you realise just how breathtaking it is. Robert, Emma and Marko had never been there before. Mum and I think that being able to come and see it once more was so special. It is a very humbling and spiritual place and I hope one day I can visit it again.

ULURU

Katherine

We got to return to Katherine to visit our friends, the Mannion family. It was great to see them, and so nice of them to show us around. They showed us a stunning cycad garden, the beautiful Edith Falls and we got to swim at Umbrawarra Gorge. It was also Harley's birthday, so we got to celebrate that with him. Thank you so much Scott, Vicki, Holly and Harley. We had such a fun time.

THE GHAN

I think that trains are one of the most fun modes of transport in the world! On our trip across Australia, hopping on the Ghan in Darwin was where our adventure began. Travelling with us was my teacher Emma and her fiancé Marko, who works in the crocodile department (yes, they're getting married soon!!!). On the three-day journey, the train made two stops for everyone to stretch their legs and look around. The first stop was in Katherine. We got to take a helicopter ride over Katherine Gorge – WOW!

It was Marko's first helicopter ride. The gorge is so beautiful and we were so lucky to be able to see it. The Ghan stopped again in Alice Springs. While we were there we got to have a beaut bonza camel ride. Emma and I rode Dock, Mum and Robert rode Salay, and Marko rode Ruby. They were so cute, I wanted to hug them and squeeze their big squishy lips. When we arrived in Adelaide we were sad to leave the train but extremely excited about our next adventure, which was to drive back to Darwin. Can you believe we crossed the continent twice, and drove 4500 kilometres?

Leaf the Kookaburra

Leaf the kookaburra was found on the road at Beerburrum after being hit by a car and was transported to the Australia Zoo Wildlife Hospital by the Australia Zoo Rescue Unit.

Dr Robyn's X-rays and assessment revealed Leaf had a fractured wing, bruising to the right eye, bleeding on the lungs and an open wound near the tail. Leaf underwent surgery to pin the fractured wing and stitch the wound closed, and was given a course of antibiotics, pain relief and anti-inflammatories.

Leaf is currently in the Bird ICU at the Australia Zoo Wildlife Hospital receiving treatment, and will be released once healed.

Happy Birthday to...
Queto the Blue and Gold Macaw

❋ Age: 7 years (DOB 27/2/2004)

❋ Gender: Male

❋ Being a macaw, Queto is not a species that you would find in the wilds of Australia. Macaws are exotic to this country, coming from parts of Central and South America where they inhabit a range of different habitat types. Macaws have two features that everyone notices; the first is their very large and powerful beak that is used to crack nuts and berries, and the other is their very long and colourful tail, which they use as a rudder and a brake when flying through the forest canopy.

Queto is still pretty young, considering macaws can live to around 70 years of age. He is probably the quietest of all the macaws here at Australia Zoo and has a very laid back nature.

MARCH MARCH MARCH

I am so passionate about the 'Bindi Wildlife Adventures' book series. We travelled to New York and LA to launch the first two books in America. I got to talk to many school groups, do many signings and talks at book stores and appear on many TV

and radio interviews. We did the *Rachael Ray Show*, *Good Morning America* and the *Absolutely Mindy* radio show, just to name a few. It was a great tour and I was so privileged to share the conservation message with such a broad audience. The books are fiction stories, based on our real life adventures. Kids from ages 6-12 (younger or older) seemed to really enjoy the series. It was nice to see kids accidentally learning something while reading them!

Book Tour

DISNEYLAND

I am officially the luckiest girl on the planet! We had a blast in Disneyland, I can't believe how awesome it was. Robert and I had to do three hours of school every day we were there, but I enjoyed reading a good book or two with plush Mickey Mouse.

Hee, hee. However, we did get to chill out with the real Mickey Mouse at his house in Toon Town. I think that it's safe to say I'm now taller than him! I also got to go on some sensational and thrilling rides. They were a screaming good time!

Mum, Robert and I also pulled some funny faces next to a billboard in Disneyland. I'm not sure what we were doing, but it was very funny.

Our whole Disney experience was awesome and filled with laughter. I hope we can go there again soon.

Shania the Red-necked Wallaby

Shania, a young female joey, was found in her mother's pouch in a backyard in Carters Ridge, north of Kenilworth. Fortunately she was uninjured, though very thin and riddled with lice. Her mother had to be euthanised as she was suffering from a severe infection in her left leg, as well as an injured left eye.

Dr Robyn administered Shania pain relief, which is what is happening in this photo, and treated her lice infestation. Vitamin E cream was also applied to Shania's skin to help it heal.

Shania is now being looked after by a registered kangaroo joey carer, who will be able to provide her with the round-the-clock feeding and care she requires. When Shania is old enough she will be released back into the wild.

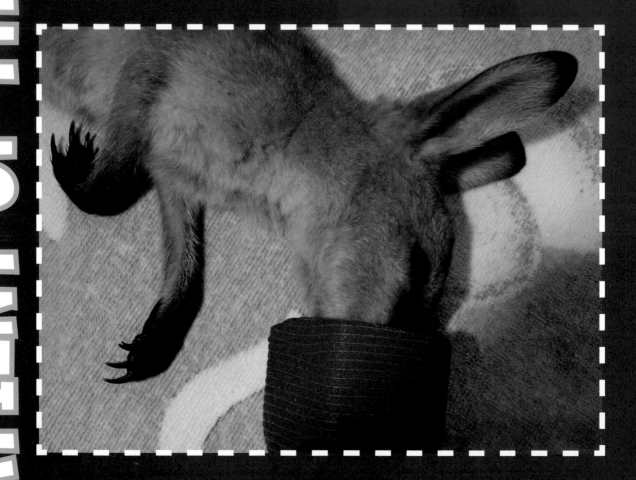

Happy Birthday to...
Bonnie the Otter

✳ Age: 13 years (DOB 4/3/1998)
✳ Gender: Female
✳ Bonnie joined our family at Australia Zoo back in 1999 as a cheeky one-year-old otter, along with her sister Maria. Bonnie enjoys a variety of food items on a daily basis at Australia Zoo, with some of her favourite foods being garfish, whiting and crayfish.

APRIL

APRIL APRIL APRIL

Australia Zoo's newest arrival was born 12 April. She is the cutest baby, with big floppy ears, huge feet and some very kissable lips . . . Did I mention she's a rhino? Savannah is a gorgeous girl and she is the first baby rhino born at Australia Zoo. She is a very curious and adventurous girl; however, if she gets scared she always runs back to her comforting mother. Savannah loves and lives for hugs and scratches. When we scratch the right spot, she turns into jelly and falls down.

Now everybody can learn more about Savannah and share our love for her, as she can now be adopted through Australia Zoo's adopt an animal program.

She is so sweet; everybody loves her!

BABY RHINO

75

CAMEL EXPERIENCE

Our two supermodel camels are drop dead gorgeous.
At Australia Zoo, everyone has a chance to meet them
and get to know their hilariously cute personalities.
Delilah and Esther have just been added to our sensational animal
encounters, where visitors don't just look at them, but get in with
them! They get to hug and kiss them and take away a beaut bonza
photo to share with everyone at home. Robert and I got to hang
with them for a photo shoot and share some delicious carrots.
Delilah and Esther are best friends and love meeting new people and
getting hugs and kisses. They are one of my favourite animals in the zoo.

OREGON

It is always so much fun to catch up with family when we go to Oregon! Our first stop together was the Sea Lion Caves. It is the largest sea cave in the world and is home to hundreds if not thousands of sea lions. I love watching the old ones sleep on the high rocks and the curious youngsters play in the deadly, crashing surf.

When we were on the beach Mum, Robert and I built a tip-top-terrific fort that could withstand a hurricane. We called it 'Fort Irwin'.

While we were on the coast, we also visited the Newport Aquarium. I made friends with a sea otter who was extremely curious and saw a shocking sculpture. It was made entirely out of beach rubbish. It is astonishing to me how wasteful people are!

ET the (Extremely Tiny*) Echidna

Poor little ET was found weakly roaming around by himself in a backyard at Maleny. He was taken to the Australia Zoo Wildlife Hospital by the concerned resident of the property.

ET was very thin and extremely weak, and much too young to be on his own. He had a bleeding tail and a blood test revealed ET was anaemic.

Dr Amber administered ET subcutaneous (under the skin) fluids and applied several heat packs to the tail end while he received a blood transfusion. ET was kept nice and warm during his overnight stay in the nursery.

ET was given to a registered wildlife carer and will return to the hospital for a check-up every week until he's well enough to be released into the wild.

Happy Birthday to...
Savannah the White Rhinoceros

❋ Age: newborn (DOB 12/04/11)
❋ Gender: Female
❋ Savannah was born weighing between 50 and 60 kilograms, which is a very healthy size for a newborn! As the first rhino to ever be born at Australia Zoo, Savannah has had a lot of attention and love lavished on her by her mum, Caballe, and everyone else at Australia Zoo!

MAY MAY MAY

Travel back in time*

WOW! I can't believe how much fun our dinosaur trip to Winton and Richmond (in Queensland) was! Not many people realise how many dinosaur discoveries have been made in Australia. However, my brother does because he is dinosaur mad, which is why Mum, Robert and I decided to mount an expedition to check out some of those amazing fossils. The highlights of our trip were going to Kronosaurus Korner in Richmond, Australian Age Of Dinosaurs just south of Winton and Lark Quarry outside Winton. It was amazing and we learnt so much. Robert was the most excited though. He says that his favourite dinosaur is an Australian species called an Australovenator, so he was ecstatic when he got to meet the fossil relics of that very dinosaur, whose name is Banjo.

We also loved it when we got to go fossicking with two fantastic palaeontologists who helped us find some unbelievable fossils. They then let us excavate them using their special tools. It was fascinating and I never knew how much patience and time it takes to excavate one tiny fossil! I admire every palaeontologist who dedicates so much of their time for the sake of learning more about Earth's remarkable past. It was a trip that we'll never forget.

Another book launch – but not mine!

Wow! I felt so privileged and honoured when Dick Smith asked me to help him launch his new book *Population Crisis* in Sydney. Dick Smith is a man who I truly look up to, and his book covers issues I am very passionate about.

Population is a subject that is the 'elephant in the room' that nobody wants to talk about. This must change. Overpopulation is the cause of most of the problems facing our planet today. At the moment our planet is home to around 7 billion people, and this number grows by about 240,000 humans being born each day. As our population continues to grow at this rapid rate, the globe's precious resources become scarcer. I believe that everyone should have the choice of family planning, and that we must open our minds and eyes for ideas to solve this population crisis now.

Slavko Footy Match

On Friday 27 May we had our annual Slavko Australia Zoo footy match. Slavko was an artist at Australia Zoo who passed away in 2005, so we have a footy match every year to remember him. He was a fantastic man and was an amazing artist. He used to give me some tips and teach me some fun art techniques. The two teams that play against each other are the Keepers and Construction. All of the players' friends and family come to watch the night and cheer for their favourite team. I always cheer for everybody though because I know all the blokes playing, so it makes it hard for me to choose one team over the other. However, my dad used to play, so I went for his team, which always won! This year the construction team won for the second year in a row. They were very excited even though they were a little battered and bruised. It was great night and all of the funds raised will go towards our annual crocodile research trip.

Asteroid the Green Sea Turtle

Asteroid the juvenile male Green Sea Turtle was found floating at Moreton Island and taken to the Australia Zoo Wildlife Hospital. Dr Robyn examined Asteroid and found he was suffering from fibropapillomas (large warts with a 'cauliflower' texture). Dr Robyn prepared Asteroid for surgery to remove the larger fibropapillomas on both front flippers, which were the ones affecting him most.

Following surgery, Dr Robyn prescribed antibiotics and anti-inflammatories to fend off any secondary infection from the fibropapillomas. Luckily Asteroid's future is positive because the growths didn't reach his lungs. He will be monitored at the Australia Zoo Wildlife Hospital for infection, and released once he returns to full health.

Fibropapillomas are affecting sea turtles worldwide; it is the only known animal disease that has spread worldwide.

Happy Birthday to...
Echo the Cheetah

* Age: 7 years (DOB 19/5/2004)
* Gender: Male
* Weight: 50kg (110lbs)
* Echo is the big man on campus. Born at DeWildt Cheetah & Wildlife Trust in South Africa, Echo is the biggest of our four cheetahs and he takes on the role of protector and big brother. He has a serious demeanour but also has a soft and playful side. He likes to use his strength and large body to wrestle with the other cheetahs. His favourite sparring partner is his brother Foxy, but the girls love to jump in and have a go too. Echo loves long naps in the shade under a tree with his handlers.

JUNE JUNE JUNE

Robert's Un-birthday

I can't believe how fast Robert is growing up. We celebrated his seven and a half birthday on 1 June. He had a great night playing with friends and family and was totally surprised to find out that it was his un-birthday, because he had completely forgotten the date! It was fantastic to watch him laugh and play and gorge himself with sweets. He was so excited to receive Mum's gift, which was a cast of the fossil skull of an allosaurus. He screamed and jumped up and down so much that it was hard to take a photo of him next to his present! I am really proud of my little brother and everything that he has achieved in seven and a half years. I am so lucky to have him in my life.

A Crocodile Soap Opera

What an action-packed weekend! We had to move one of our saltwater crocodiles, Agro, from his earth pond at Australia Zoo because he is getting older, and we didn't want him to be cold during the winter months. Agro and his girlfriend Cookie had to be moved into Shaka and Cassie's warm pond. Shaka and Cassie, however, weren't getting along as well as they should've been, so we had to move Cassie in with Bluey, who is another one of our saltwater crocs. Then we put Shaka into Agro and Cookie's earth pond. It is all kind of like one big croc soap opera! Everything ran smoothly. Robert and I got to help by being on the jump team with the crocs. That means we all line up and jump on the crocodile – it looks like a stack of dominos falling down. This method is best for the crocodile and doesn't hurt them. It's kind of like a bunch of marshmallows jumping on a chunk of steel!! All of the crocs are doing really well and are very happy in their new ponds.

The APPLE ISLE

Our trip to Tasmania has to be one of the best trips of my life! Mum, Robert, our Aunt Bonnie and Uncle John, and our friends Shelley, Hannah and Harley came with us on this fantastic adventure. We got to do so many fun things! We started off in Marrawah where we went Tasmanian devil watching. It was nice to find out how they're going. They are having a hard time coping with a facial tumour disease that is wiping them out at a rapid rate. This disease is one of two known contagious cancers, and it's spreading from devil to devil throughout Tasmania. At Australia Zoo, we are part of a mainland breeding program for the devils. Hopefully the devils can be protected, so that we don't lose them forever. The next place we visited on our amazing journey was Strahan. There we ate a lot of cheese, and got to go on a fun train ride and a Gordon River Boat Cruise to Sarah Island. That was very interesting and we learnt a lot. Our last stop was Cradle Mountain. So beautiful! While we were there it snowed, so of course we had some massive and epic snowball battles, and we built a cool snowman. It was a trip that will remember forever. Tasmania is one of my favourite places in Australia.

Russel the pelican*

Poor Russel was found at a caravan park in Noosaville, entangled in fishing line. Briano and James from the Australia Zoo Rescue Unit took him back to the Australia Zoo Wildlife Hospital where he was assessed by Dr Amber.

She found him to be bright and responsive even though there was a fishing hook embedded in his left wing, causing some trauma to the membrane, and his right leg had an indentation from the fishing line wrapped tightly around it.

Dr Amber anaesthetised Russel so she could carefully remove the hook from his wing and untangle the fishing line from around his body. After the operation he was put on antibiotics to help his wing heal.

Russel is now recovering in the company of other pelicans with local registered seabird carers. He will return for a check-up and if Dr Amber is happy with his progress, Russel the pelican will be released back into the wild.

Happy Birthday to...
Djagarna the Black-necked Jabiru

❋ Age: 7 years (DOB 30/6/2004)
❋ Gender: Female
❋ Djagarna is a beautiful female jabiru, more commonly known as a black-necked stork. She was born at the Rainforest Habitat in Port Douglas in 2004 and came to live at Australia Zoo when she was three months old. Djagarna is the star of our daily Free Flight Bird Show.

Adults at kids prices!

Home of The Crocodile Hunter

Present this voucher at Australia Zoo before 31 December 2012 to receive this ripper offer!

WINNER 2008 AUSTRALIAN TOURISM AWARDS MAJOR TOURIST ATTRACTIONS

Open every day 9:00am - 5:00pm *(Closed Christmas Day, ANZAC Day open 1:30pm - 5:30pm)*
Steve Irwin Way, Beerwah, Sunshine Coast, QLD 4519 info@australiazoo.com.au Ph: (07) 5436 2000

QUEENSLAND TOURISM AWARDS 2009 Hall of Fame

www.australiazoo.com.au